Rebecca Crompto
and
Elizabeth Grace Thomson

PIONEERS OF STITCHERY IN THE 1930s

BERYL DEAN WITH PAMELA PAVITT

Acknowledgements

We are sincerely indebted to Thelma Nye for her invaluable advice and for so generously editing this book; also to Joan Edwards for the benefit of her opinion and help. We wish to express very real gratitude to the owners of Rebecca Crompton's work, who have so kindly allowed examples to be reproduced. Especial thanks to members of her family, Monique Francis, Rebecca Speakman and Tony Soar for their kindness; also to Susan Olumide and Diana Bottoms.

We gratefully acknowledge Derby Museum and Art Gallery for the transparency of *Adam and Eve* and wish to thank Elizabeth Spencer, Keeper of Decorative Art, and Diana Moss; also Pickford's House Museum for their help. Thanks also to the University of Derby and College of Art, Derby, for permission to reproduce examples of Rebecca Crompton's embroidery. The photograph of Bromley School of Art is reproduced by permission of Muriel Searle. By courtesy of the Board of Trustees of the Victoria and Albert Museum, three examples are included. We are most grateful to the Embroiderers' Guild, Hampton Court Palace, who have given their support and have kindly loaned transparencies of M.E.G. Thomson's embroideries. The illustration of machine embroidery designed by Rebecca Crompton has been supplied by the Dorking Branch.

Our sincere gratitude is offered to Betty Keeling and to Madame Sheeta. We acknowledge BT. Batsford Ltd. for permission to reproduce four illustrations from Rebecca Crompton's 1936 publication, *Modern Design in Embroidery.* We appreciate being able to include the contemporary reminiscences of Rebecca Crompton's early life recalled by her friend Edith M. Woods.

We are indebted to the following for their excellent photographs:

Cameracraft of Aylesbury and Hemel Hempstead

Croydon Local Studies Library

Ron and Phill Davies, Aberaevon, Dyfed

Dudley Moss, Stanmore, Middlesex and *The World of Embroidery*

David Patterson, Brandon, Norfolk

Tom Hill, University of Derby

John MacRae, Apex Photography, Loughborough

BD and PP, London, 1996

First published 1996

ISBN 0 9528273 01

Printed in Great Britain by Waterloo Printing Company Limited
5 Baron's Place, Waterloo Road, London SE1 8XB
Published by Beryl Dean, London

Pickford's House Museum has set up a national register of the work of Rebecca Crompton with the aim to record the current whereabouts of each piece. Please contact The Keeper of Decorative Art, 41 Friarsgate Derby DE1 1DA, telephone: 01332 255363

Nursery panel, c 1931

Setting the Scene - up to the 1930s

People today who are inspired by creative stitchery and take textiles seriously, may not realise how much originated with the innovative approach of Rebecca Crompton in the early 1930s. She changed the direction of the development of design for embroidery, and it was the teaching of Elizabeth Thomson which made it more widely known and understood.

Among traditionalists the introduction of this new 'Ultra Modern' approach aroused much controversy. To understand this reaction the characteristics of decorative needlework in the late 19th and early 20th centuries must be considered, then the difference of outlook will become apparent. The emphasis had been almost entirely upon the perfection of technique (it was not unknown for a judge to examine first the neatness of the back of a piece of work). The use of an embroidery frame (an aid to prevent puckering) was regarded as something of a status symbol! The knowledge of stitches and methods were very extensive, but this concentration upon technique was at the expense of interest in creativity and originality of design, which was but little encouraged. Transfers were commonly used and generally these were repeating patterns or symmetrical decoration. The origin of a design was unimportant and many were copied or adapted from traditional sources. Of course there were notable exceptions. There were handsome hangings, bedspreads, portieres, and these compositions, for example, might be carried out entirely in drawn thread and pulled work using natural linen threads. Or perhaps the sheer exploitation of a technique, such as fine white work could produce examples of intriguing charm. Satin stitch and long and short stitch were employed to execute the elaborate figurative and floral subjects, where the aim was to attain realism. For this, filo-floss silk, filoselle silk or crewel wool was used because the long ranges of tone obtainable facilitated graduation of colour in stitchery, so essential for expressing the design of the time. This was an end in itself and almost the ultimate purpose of existence! Comparatively little interest was taken in colour, although all shades of green were very popular. The fabrics used were mainly linen, crêpe-de-chine, cotton backed satin or serge, many of which had smooth surfaces. Contrast of texture was not appreciated. Concurrently with this concentration upon technique, there were artists with imagination who were interested in expressing their ideas in terms of fabric, but were of limited technical ability and knowledge, therefore had to depend upon appliqué, which, through lack of stitchcraft, they just sewed down the cut edges. But with the introduction of interesting colour schemes this approach continued to develop, particularly in the Art Schools of Scotland.

With the publication of Mrs Christie's *Samplers and Stitches*, in 1920, the decorative quality of stitches was appreciated and extended. But still it was rare for more than one technique (for example, laid-work) to be used to carry out a piece of work. Things were moving forward. There was at this time, in Derby, a young girl, Rebecca, who was very excited about the embroideries she was doing. Little could the influence that she would exert in the future have then been foreseen.

Rebecca Crompton

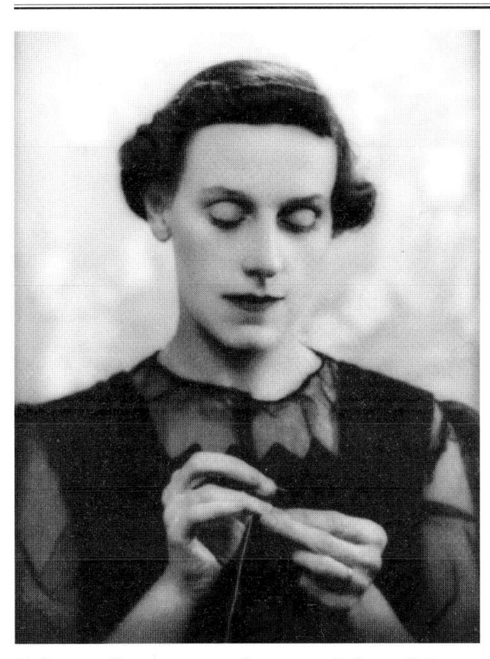

Rebecca Crompton at the age of about 26

SCHOOLDAYS

The Soar family lived in Derby, with the father being an office worker for the LMS Railway. The children were Harry, Mary, Rebecca, Jane and Lydia. Rebecca was born on 7th August 1895. She was educated at the school which became Parkfield Cedars Grammar School where she shone as being outstandingly gifted. Her headmistress, Miss Jean Keay, and the Art mistress, Miss K. M. Warren, were keenly interested in needlework and design: this must have influenced and encouraged the spark of originality that 'Becky' Soar possessed. She was able to experiment with the fabrics which the school provided, such as hessian, linen and towelling, which was an unusual mixture for those days. The staff gave her great encouragement recognising her aptitude for design and embroidery. But she could be mischievous. On one occasion she was caught drawing on the lid of her desk. She was duly 'told off' but the drawing was considered to be very good. At another time she was sitting in the back row surreptitiously working a border during a scripture lesson; she was hauled to the front. 'What are you doing Becky Soar?' She had made Miss Keay a small bag worked in Romanian stitch.

Her school days showed Becky as a lively pupil, bubbling over with enthusiasm and a friendly attitude to everyone. She took a keen interest in everything and everybody. Suddenly, on a country walk, she would dash home to draw a design based on something she had seen. She had a strong feeling for colour and movement. It was always the same; ideas crowding into her imaginative mind which needed to be expressed with great urgency. She had a tremendous capacity for work but with her sensitive nature she was very emotional and highly strung.

FRIENDS AND FABRICS

Two particular factors must have had a great influence upon her. One was the friendship which her teacher had with Ann Macbeth, the very accomplished and well known embroiderer, who was interested in school children being taught decorative stitchery using bright colours. She wrote on craftwork subjects and was head of her department at Glasgow School of Art, which was important in the Art Nouveau Movement in Scotland. She often visited a relative at 'Macbeth's' antique shop on Derby Market Street. She would also see her friend at the Parkfield Cedars School, sometimes with her pupils and showed great interest in their craftwork. What excitement it must have been to a schoolgirl to meet such an experienced and understanding embroiderer. Apparently Becky herself once finished a panel which Ann Macbeth had started and left behind in the school: this was to hang in the hall for many years.

The other factor was the arrival of a huge hamper from an aunt who had visited Romania. Her sister Jane wrote: 'We children were thrilled, it was full of the most exciting and lovely things - wall hangings, woven and embroidered by the peasants - beautiful carpets in brilliant colours and the finest lawn cloths exquisitely worked around the borders. Amongst all this was a length of white hand woven crêpe material with a border of peasant embroidery worked with orange and red floss silk which she unpicked to find out how it had been worked. She then completed the border'.

ART STUDENT AND TEACHER

In 1913, Rebecca started studying at Derby School of Art in Green Lane. Here she worked for what was then the Board of Education's Drawing examination becoming a competent draughtswoman in the process. This course included many aspects of drawing. She had already studied for the City and Guilds Embroidery Certificates, winning a Bronze medal. Her time at the Art School also included the study of dress design and making, plus all that entails. By 1916 she had taken and passed the Board of Education's examinations.

Becky made herself original clothes. Her friend from Derby School of Art, Edith M. Wood, remembered a vivid red outfit which she had enhanced by adding embroidery on the bodice and another dress of white cotton with stitched decoration round the skirt.

Her first teaching post was at Northampton School of Art, where she was appointed in 1917. Her classes covered a variety of subjects: drawing from the antique and perspective, dress design and all aspects of embroidery. A member of the office staff of those days still remembered the brightly colourful embroidery on her dresses.

The HMI (His Majesty's Inspector), F. W. Burrows, was so impressed with the work produced by her students that he borrowed many samples to show to other schools of art. This was the beginning of an important influence upon her future. He was a perceptive man who could see the latent potentials of many teachers, thus helping and guiding them in their careers. In the course of visiting Art Schools he continued to keep in touch with Rebecca's progress. Her personality and presence made a great impact upon staff and students. 'She was so different from other teachers and had a delightful giggle.'

It was at Northampton Art School that Rebecca Soar met Oswald Crompton, many years her senior, who was a lecturer, painter, water colourist and craftsman in enamel work. They were married before he took up his appointment as Principal of Croydon School of Art, Surrey, in 1923.

Sampler, 13.5 in. x 10 in., c 1932

'Girl with Hoop' Appliqué

'Veiled Petals', sampler 10 in. square, worked in buttonhole stitches

'June', small panel 12 in. square

CROYDON SCHOOL OF ART

The Art School had been founded in 1868, a somewhat independent Institution receiving its first Croydon Council grant in 1895, and was finally taken over by Croydon Council in 1932. The premises which were used for the classes by staff and students were above the Public Hall at the crossroads in the centre of the town. (Since World War II this area has been completely remodelled and is quite different from pre-war days). The Art School entrance was up a darkish, rather 'smelly' (so said a student!) staircase to the rooms, where, from the 'life' class it was possible to look down through a window and see the stage of the theatre of the Public Hall. The premises were surprisingly unprepossessing and the conditions in which the students worked were cramped and somewhat inconvenient, even the corridors being used for private study periods. Students had to work hard, evenings included. A typical day was 9am to 1pm, 2 pm to 4pm, 7pm to 9pm. There was a tea club which included soft drinks, bread and butter and jam, with any profits going to buy cakes for special occasions! In their free time student-teachers would often work with full-time students. There was also a great willingness for students to help one another - in fact there was a great camaraderie among them all.

At one time, Rebecca had a day off a week and on some of these occasions she left her own, sometimes 'scribbled', design on a piece of paper for the embroidery students to interpret, usually on a linen background. Sometimes they would work a motif that had been noted during museum study, not necessarily from an embroidery piece, maybe something from a pottery pattern or wood carving. This would be adapted for an embroidery design and worked out in stitchery, possibly for the corner of a tray cloth or the side of a tea cosy.

Croydon School of Art. This area is now completely changed

HER TEACHING

Rebecca Crompton taught embroidery and dress design at Croydon and she joined classes for dressmaking, tailoring and lace making. Joan Dukes, who was on the staff says: 'At that time Mrs Crompton still wore peasant style dress with colourful embroidery, which was copied by the students. She was full of vitality and brimful of ideas. It was some time later that she began to experiment with a freer use of embroidery, combining appliqué with surface stitchery in an entirely new, original and very personal way, which was her own creation. She should be regarded as the originator of revolutionary methods and free design. She was an inspiration to all who worked with her and her classes were overflowing with students'.

She was a versatile teacher who took classes in drawing as well as her specialities. She introduced the millinery teacher, Madame Sheeta, who she asked on one occasion to make a hat in the shape of a butterfly. This was to add another aspect to the students' course: always vital to her teaching.

At about this time Constance Howard went to Croydon School of Art to visit Mrs Crompton. She commented upon her strong personality and charm: 'I could talk to her quite easily. I had heard of her reputation - that she was a dragon in the class room, and that if you were late she ignored you for the day, also if you didn't work: and that she was a brilliant teacher, which indeed she was'. One way in which she taught design was by using torn paper of different tones. These were arranged on a background stressing simplicity of form and freedom of line. `She showed how an embroideress can become a creative artist instead of being merely a copyist.' Other past Croydon students have observed that: 'Her freedom of design and use of threads and colour opened up a whole new way of working. Without her influence and example the qualities and excitement of textiles which she created would never have been discovered'. 'Rebecca Crompton got embroidery out of a rut and changed the circle.' A colleague commented that: 'Design was important to her: she was a catalyst: interested in colour: an excellent artist, with sensitivity and energy'. It was she who first used red and magenta or cerise together, and it took time to become acceptable.

Genevieve Marriott, a student at Croydon, said: 'Mrs Crompton made two small sketches on the side of one of my drawings, when trying to make me "loosen up" my work. I remember the impact this had on me, her quick movement with the pencil - making the cock really crow!'.

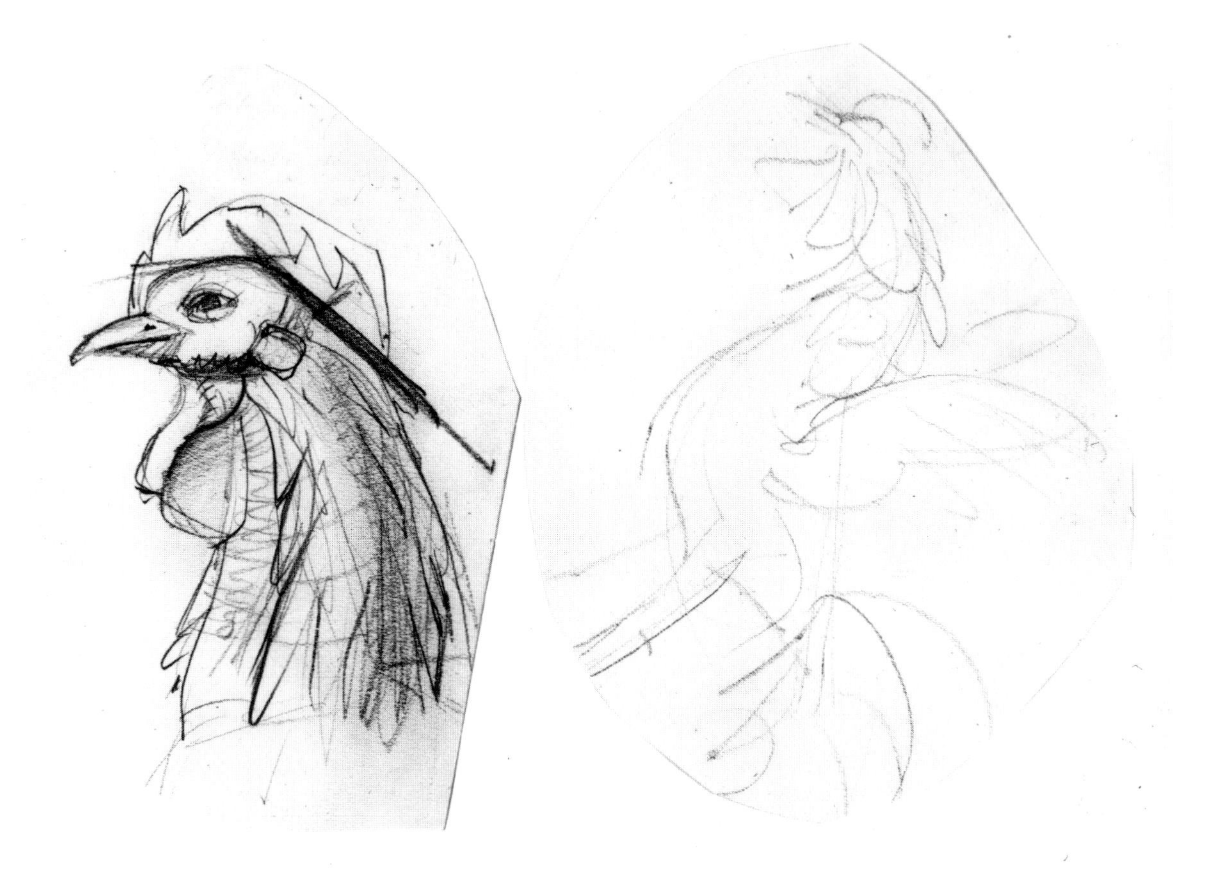

Small sketch (right) made by Rebecca Crompton on the side of Genevieve Marriot's drawing

A GREAT PERSONALITY

Rebecca Crompton was well-known in and around Croydon itself for her style of dress. One well remembered outfit was a big cloak and cap in red, green and blue. A member of staff at Croydon recalls her colourful embroidered peasant style dresses. 'She was difficult to fit when new clothes were being made for her and would "panic" when taking clothes off over her head. She always dressed well, her outfits suited her personality and figure. She liked her students to look smart too.' They were very much influenced by her

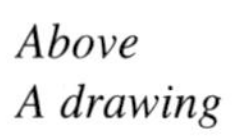

Above
A drawing

Top right
'Autumn Pavement'
Wall panel mainly appliqué, c 1931

Right
A painting

and one of them can remember persuading her mother to take her into the local department store to buy fabrics in similar colours to those in the clothes her teacher was wearing.

STUDENTS

All the while, work was continuing in the classes at Croydon School of Art. Doris Anwyn brought a piece of embroidery, worked at her day school, when she was interviewed by the Principal to become an art student. Seeing it, he said: 'better join HER class!'. SHE, referring to Rebecca Crompton, is remembered as 'someone apart', a near genius with such vision. There was something special about the way she dressed (apparently her clothes had become more sophisticated by this time). Helen Sandys remembers that her course included heraldry, history of ornament, visits to museums, drawing, design and practical embroidery. As her studies progressed she says: '...light gradually dawned as to what embroidery really was ...'. Another student remembers that Rebecca took students for the memory drawing examination. 'Once I was asked to draw a rearing horse, another time children playing with dogs. I remember seeing the work of the advanced students for the Industrial Design Examination in Embroidery. They asked to study with Rebecca as she had become renowned for her very personal and creative approach to embroidery and some exciting and beautiful work was produced.'

An example of the effect which can be achieved by the use of simple stitchery

EXHIBITIONS

An exhibition of embroidery held at the Art School in 1925 was commented on in the *Embroideress* magazine (priced 1/- per copy). The reviewer, E. R. says: 'that to visit it on a day of rain and wind was to prove oneself, to some extent, independent of the weather, for, on going into the small room where the needlework was arranged, such a shining of fresh clear colour met one's eyes as to make the lack of sunshine outside seem of no great account. The works were neatly executed and carried out in a wise economical way both as to stitches and material. The teacher was Mrs Crompton and her students knew how to work hard, "for those who were only able to attend evening classes had several good pieces to their credit". Giving an insight into the teaching method in Croydon classes, it was noted that the samplers were worked concurrently with their other pieces as they wanted to learn new stitches. Thus the exhibition included samplers, panels and articles such as cushions, bags, luncheon mats and dresses: one was in holland fabric with a deep blue linen hem, which was repeated around the neck and on the sleeves. Another eye-catching exhibit was a red woollen rep cap with jade green and natural wool embroidery. Bright pure colour schemes had been used on many exhibits, all rather too similar, it was thought, many "singing their loudest"!'

The embroidery being created on the Continent was exciting and in the later twenties and early thirties a German magazine *Stickerein und Spitzen* was eagerly perused by Rebecca and her students, the latter were sometimes known to hide it under their desks so that she did not know they had it!

She often designed her own unique frames to surround her panels: some having mirror or filigree work incorporated in them. The Rowley Gallery of Kensington Church Street, London, would make these up for her.

Rebecca Crompton with her panel 'Yellow Dog' while on show at The Redfern Gallery, London

A WIDER WORLD

Later Rebecca Crompton was appointed part-time Inspector for the Board of Education. By 1930 she had become an examiner for the Industrial Design examination in Embroidery and Women's Crafts set by the Board of Education (this was the body that organised and administered the examinations undertaken by Art Schools). She was also examiner in Embroidery for the Lancashire and Cheshire Institute and the Birmingham Educational Union, and was involved in the City and Guilds of London Institute.

Rebecca's own work was widely exhibited and well known outside the Art Schools, and examples completed at the end of the twenties now find a place of honour at the Victoria and Albert Museum (textile students' room). In his book *Ornament* (published 1986), Stuart Durand illustrates two of these pieces now in the Museum, as typical examples of that period, along with wallpapers and textile designs, book illustrations, lettering and decorative pieces. In the chapter on 'Modernism', one panel entitled *Diana* is illustrated. It is worked in organdie, with a footnote that Diana is no longer considered the huntress of old, a goddess, but shown as a devotee of physical fitness; the other was *The Magic Garden*, using appliqué and coloured silks, a much more staid figure with movement all around her. (In a previous chapter of the same book, a piece by Ann Macbeth is illustrated.)

'SOMEONE APART'

By working tremendously hard, Rebecca was producing many increasingly interesting examples of her own work. A contemporary observed 'her insight also her foresight formed the basis for many embroideries of the following decades because she was such an excellent artist'. Another colleague said: 'she lived in a world of innovation and spontaneity'. Her approach to design was unrestrained, the drawing was free in style, using simple motifs. There was characteristic movement in the line. She played with the fabrics until the best arrangement had been achieved. She was a stickler for good technique and became absorbed in planning the methods to use. She was 'crazy on interlacing stitch but was defeated by Russian drawn ground'. Her particular innovation was the appreciation of contrasting textures and the use of transparent materials (which we take for granted today). 'She used ribbons, braids, net, studs, beads and buttons on anything! A real 20th century pioneer.' Her husband commented on the masses and masses of buttons she put on her embroidery, 'but none on my shirts'. She would work late into the night if necessary, revelling in varied fabrics and stitchery. She also introduced the use of striped and checked gingham and spotted cottons as a means of making designs by contriving various arrangements, with the addition of stitchery.

SADNESS

In 1930 their only child Phyllida, who used to spend her holidays on the Continent with her cousins, tragically died there at the age of eight as a result of complications following scarlet fever. That her mother was in England added to their grief. Rebecca changed completely, becoming rather haggard and thin. She had given up her picturesque dress and, as Joan Dukes recalls 'she became very French and chic, though still original and unusual'.

MEETING GRACE THOMSON

It was at about this time that she met Grace Thomson (known as Grace then, though later she used her other name, Elizabeth). It was an important meeting for the world of embroidery. Grace, a trained painter, had a post in a school in Kingswood, near Croydon.

Among other aspects of art she wanted to teach the children embroidery and enrolled as a student at Croydon Art School. It was exciting for Rebecca to have such a gifted artist and keen stitchery student in her class. So started an interesting and stimulating collaboration, with Grace actually living for a while in the Crompton's house in Selcroft Road, Addiscombe, Croydon.

THE AUTHOR

The early thirties were an extremely busy time for Rebecca. She continued part time teaching and 'seemed to take life in a breathless way. Typical of her speed of living and working was the way she would "dash off a note" on any scrap of paper'. Never sparing herself she was writing articles, contributing to schools' pamphlets and compiling books. She lectured at Schools of Art and at the Royal College of Art, also at the V & A Museum in 1932, and at the same time was producing exciting panels, many being large pieces of work.

Her twelve-page leaflet of words and drawings, *A plea for Freedom* (1933) was written 'to encourage more liveliness and

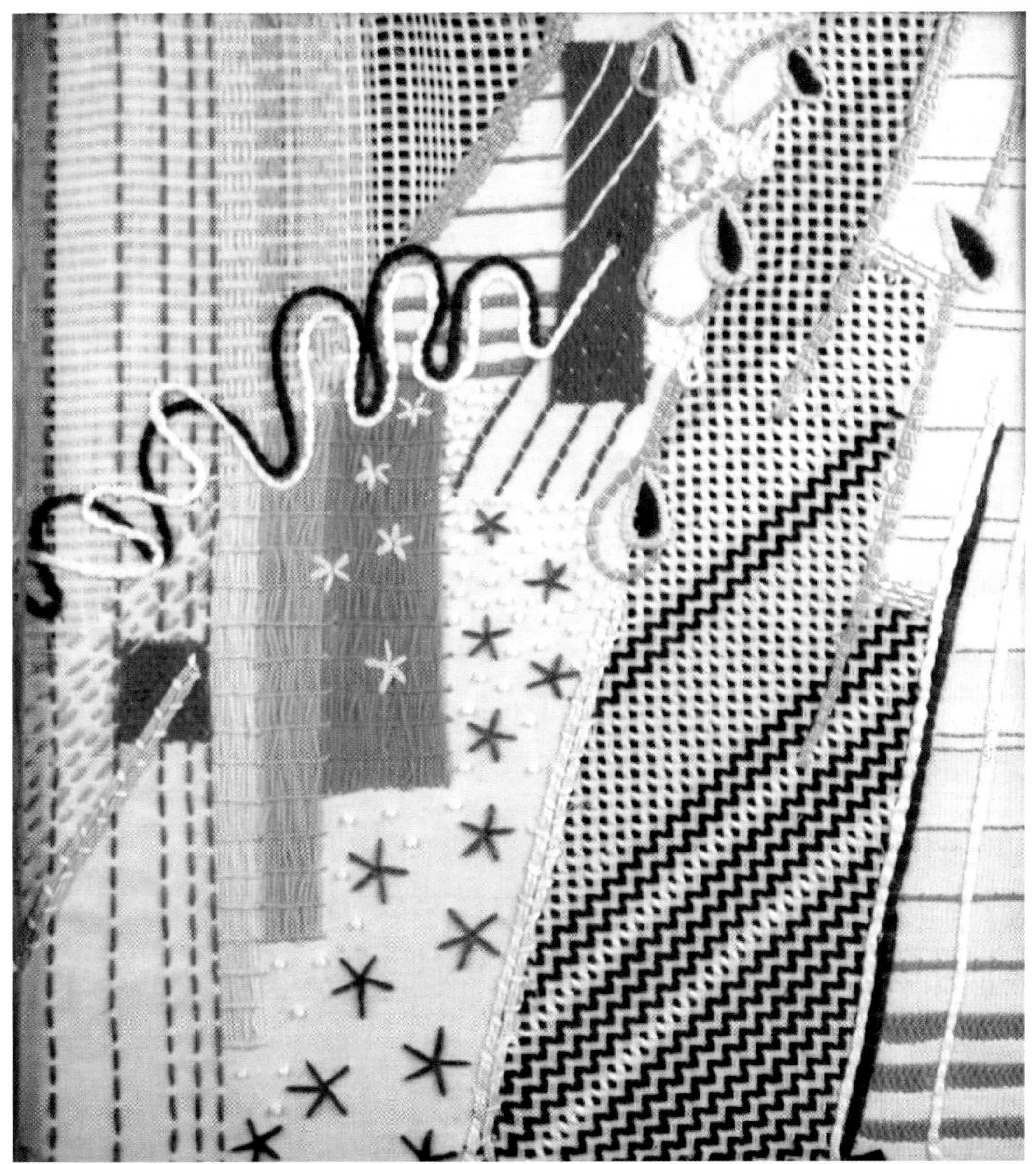

'Celebration' Number 6, 18 in. x 16.5 in. Embroidery depending upon the weave of the fabric. University of Derby

vitality in the work done by children and others'. She stressed that extreme neatness was not always a good thing and that it was an excellent idea to draw freely with a pen or brush, not necessarily from memory, continual reference could be made to actual objects. Repetition for borders or other patterns might be developed and linear forms added. Tone and half-tone could be achieved by the use of spots, stripes and lattice patterns. Vitality and inventiveness must always be expressed.

Her section in *Modern Needlecraft*, edited by Davide Minter, was a comprehensive introduction to design and stitchery showing a number of methods of embroidery, ending with decorative edges, cords and tassels. (Ann Macbeth also wrote a section in that book.) This was followed the next year by a similar team working on another book entitled *Modern Home Crafts*. Rebecca's section was 'To Inspire Original Design'. It guided the readers to an appreciation of line, tone, texture and balance, all the things she felt so important which she had imparted personally to the students in her classes.

It was also in 1933 that Mary Hogarth edited a book in which she selected recent work of English and Continental craftsmen. She reminded the readers that a new school of design had been growing up in Northern and Central Europe (which had been given impetus by the Paris Exhibition of 1925). Mary Hogarth based the pieces of embroidery illustrated in her book on the exhibition at the V & A, London, which was held in 1932 and was organised by the British Institute of Industrial Art. She selected work by Rebecca Crompton and Grace Thomson together with others worked by people who had been connected with Croydon Art School. Each page had a photograph (unfortunately, typically for those days, most were in black and white) and written detailed descriptions of the techniques and colours used. Some were panels, others articles such as pochettes, stooltops and firescreens.

RETIREMENT FROM CROYDON

It was in the summer of 1935 that both Rebecca and Oswald Crompton offered their resignations, subsequently moving from Croydon to Ealing. The following brief extracts from the minutes of 27th June 1935 of the Education Committee (School of Art Sub-Committee) show the respect in which they were held in Croydon.

'... Resignation to take effect at the end of the present term of Mrs R. Crompton, Visiting

Teacher in Embroidery and Dress Design' ... and so to advertise for a successor ..... The Sub-Committee requested the Chairman to convey to Mrs Crompton an expression of appreciation of the eminently satisfactory manner in which she had carried out her duties.'

Also the Chairman reported that Mr Oswald Crompton RMS, ARCA, proposed to terminate his engagement as Principal on 31.12.35. The Chairman was authorised to convey to Mr Crompton an expression of the Committee's great appreciation of his work as Principal for a period of over 15 years and of their gratification with the particularly satisfactory examination results achieved by pupils in the school.

When the post was advertised for Mr Crompton's successor, it was stated that the salary would be £700 per annum, rising in two stages in two years to £800. There were 72 applicants and George Frederick Hinchliff ARCA from Guildford School of Art came to Croydon in January 1936. From the minutes of 10th October 1935, the appointment was made of Miss Valerie Bayford as Visiting Teacher in Dress Design and Embroidery, for 11 hours per week at a salary of 8 shillings an hour.

SHORT COURSES

Life was still full and exciting - work to be done on a book, and courses to be organised and implemented. A teacher met her on a Saturday course for elementary teachers, when Rebecca travelled to Leicestershire. She remembers they were given fabric and the coloured threads to work with and told to make their own designs. Her colours really shocked them (a variety of very bright colours) and the ideas of one's own designs to be drawn was very daunting!

The Board of Education (as it was then) put on intensive short courses for teachers from Schools of Art. The Chief Inspector, also F. W. Burrows the Senior Inspector took a great interest in these courses, it was a privilege to be selected. The venue being London it was usually at the Central School of Arts and Crafts (as it was then known), or either the Imperial Institute or Bradleys. Those who attended came from all over the country and were thrilled to see the shops and fashion shows. There were interesting visits and lectures.

Rebecca Crompton was in charge of Dress Design, and Elizabeth Thomson, Embroidery, they alternated each year, and Madame Sheeta took millinery. These courses were an

'Fantasy', 22 in. x 17 in., showing a loose type of technique. Victoria and Albert Museum

'The Snowman', 3.5 ft x 2.5 ft, large wall panel showing textures created in cutwork and couching in contrast with the plain white background

Machine embroided mat by Dorothy Benson, designed by Rebecca Crompton

An experimental piece

experience of unforgettable value, possibly a little overwhelming at first, but soon everyone would be fired with enthusiasm for new ideas and for the gorgeous materials obtainable in London. The importance of good technique was emphasised and the work of the more experienced students was demonstrated as examples. Constance Howard said that she found Mrs Crompton 'both charming and inspiring as a teacher. With her guidance I produced a dress of striped organza that I thought beautiful! She tended to pin things up on us without cutting the fabric to show us ideas and we could cut the patterns from them'.

A teacher, who later became an Inspector herself, remembers one such course and still possesses the embroidery which she worked under Rebecca's guidance. She also did some dress designing. 'I well remember the dress she wore and her asking us all to draw what we thought the back was like.' Another teacher commented: 'Who could not be excited by her personality with such a lively and refreshing approach to craftwork so different from what had been seen before'.

The people doing embroidery found that they had to think in new ways, and the demands upon the students' imagination were at first daunting, the subjects upon which the designs were to be based had probably never been contemplated before, but with encouragement any reluctance was overcome.

Both instructors made a point of wearing very smart, individual clothes for these courses. Actually, physically they were rather alike.

MODERN EMBROIDERY DESIGN

The book *Modern Design in Embroidery* written by Rebecca Crompton, published by Batsford in 1936, was about approaching design and showed numerous line drawings and also cut paper shapes together with many photographs of her work. Davide Minter in her Foreword wrote of 'embroidery, like a phoenix of old, emerging from the fire of the centuries, glorious and with new life'. Rebecca herself reminded readers that nature does not have monotonous regularity and that design goes hand in hand with actual work and technique. At the time of publication there were few books to stimulate students' imagination. Many were all in black and white with very few photographs. But *her* book *did* make a great impact and contained colour plates, and 10 years after publication it still continued to do so.

A student at Harrogate Art School, Enid

Exercises in tone value, 8.25 in. x 7.25 in.

Mason, working with her tutor Evelyn Woodcock, who herself had been taught by Rebecca, still felt that influence by the drawings and writings in the book. All her early work, she says, was based on ideas from it. 'I remember making a pink three-sided coffee cosy with machined ric-rac braid on it and some buttons. Also a stool top for the Intermediate Examination depicting a bird flying out of a cage. I would spend hours and hours rearranging paper shapes in a given area until a balanced design was achieved'. These opinions were obviously not unanimous, especially concerning the book. Constance Howard produced the following quote: 'Unfortunately her book, so far in advance of its time, had bad reviews, which were very upsetting to her'. Subsequent to its publication, there was an exhibition at the Batsford Gallery in North Audley Street, London. It is interesting to compare the materials and stitchery she used in producing the work exhibited with that which was done at the beginning of the century, it shows how versatile Rebecca Crompton was. There were 126 items of her work, mostly decorative panels, also samplers with a few made-up articles.

Rebecca's contributions to the *Schoolmaster and Women Teachers' Chronicle* (for the National Union of Teachers) were working

'Cash in Hand', 12.5 in. x 14 in. Contrasting tones. Appliqué and stitching with the sewing machine

drawings and instructions for children to create lively samples in the classroom: they made a useful series of articles and pictures in the school syllabus. These weekly articles stopped at the outbreak of war in 1939.

Rebecca's work was exhibited at the Victoria and Albert Museum where previously it had caused a sensation, so unfamiliar were the designs and materials. In 1937 an exhibition was held at the Derby Art Gallery and another posthumously. Many of her panels were shown at the Leicester Galleries, Graves in Sloane Street and other galleries.

A DYNAMIC PERSONALITY

An underlying theme was expressed in all Rebecca Crompton's work, it was that original ideas should belong to the present. This contemporary spirit can be observed in the many panels exhibited. To mention a few: *Autumn Pavement*, in this a penny bus ticket and a comb lie beside the fallen leaves. Tennis was the theme for a design of a girl with a racquet and ball, executed in pattern darning on net. 'She was a good sportswoman and very keen on tennis. Her skating was almost to Olympic standard: she and Oswald enjoyed skating at Streatham Ice Rink.' These interests formed the subjects of several examples of her work. *Le Printemps* is another inspired piece, full of movement, which Derby College of Art own. Also the experimental panel *The Creation of Flowers* which was composed of two layers of transparent gauze embroidered and mounted half inch apart. This idea was a truly original innovation much copied at the time and continues to be today. Some of the smaller examples were based on the exploitation of one colour or one technique. For the little panel *Simplicity*. Richelieu was the method used. Another was carried out entirely in

'Le Printemps', 53 in. x 72 in., mainly appliqué.
University of Derby

Design worked on transparent gauze by means of appliqué and stitchery in fine white and black cottons. Two layers of embroidery placed together with a space of half an inch between each layer, 2 ft x 3 ft

long and short stitch. There was an immense variation of approach which showed her powers of draughtsmanship, mastery of technique and the importance she attached to finish. That Rebecca's important contribution to the history of stitched fabrics is recognised was foreseen by a friend of her girlhood, who said: 'even looking back to her school days, she was a prophet, already preoccupied with the work that was to make her famous'.

'Simplicity', 6 in. x 5 in., c 1930. An example of simple cutwork on white linen using coloured threads

A book published in 1939, *Needlework in Education* by Theodora Graham, gives an interesting look back to earlier in the thirties. In the section on embroidery she quotes fully from a 1936 comment in the *Manchester Guardian* about the new Institute of Education, London University building in Malet Street, designed by Charles Holden. He had experimented with cutting into the surface of the Portland stone in various ways to see how daylight was refracted (vertical lines also had a use to guide water running down and keeping the face of the stone clean). This variation of the way the light can somewhat change the colour and tone of the stone was compared with the self-coloured embroidered panels which Rebecca had often worked. Theodora Graham, says: 'stitchery is divided into four types - flat, looped, chained and knotted stitches, that is, from smooth to very rough. Just as the channels cut in the Portland stone give radiance to the surface, so the twists and knots of threads refract the light'. Apparently students commented on this when visiting an exhibition of Mrs Crompton's embroidery. They looked very carefully and were surprised that it was all worked in ivory silk - in one light looking almost yellow, in another mauvish.

Design planned chiefly for striking effect of tone values.
Worked in rug wool on hand-woven fabric, 4 ft x 3 ft

MORE MACHINE EMBROIDERY

Towards the end of their time at Croydon Rebecca was becoming interested in the possibilities of machine embroidery. She had frequently incorporated lines worked by the sewing machine with hand stitching. She observed how the use of a hoop extended the scope when using a domestic treadle machine for a really free line could be achieved. It is said that she never really worked the machines as she would have liked, being 'too restless for the concentration required to master the technique'. It certainly was difficult to do satin stitch and zigzag without a swing needle, only by manipulating the fabric to and fro.

Grace Thomson introduced Rebecca to the Embroidery Department of Singer's in Great Portland Street, London. The speed suited her free linear design.

The 15th Anniversary Exhibition was held by the Art and Crafts Exhibition at the Royal Academy, London (1937). In one part of the catalogue it reads: '...All exhibits in these cases have been designed by Mrs Rebecca Crompton for machine execution by the Embroidery Department of the Singer Sewing Machine Company Inc'. It was the first time that the Judges had accepted machine embroidery in such an exhibition.

Singer's welcomed Rebecca to work in the department whenever she liked to visit, and were gratified that Schools of Art were wanting to know of the possibilities of the machine as a medium of expression in embroidery and a year or so before the war some schools were having trade machines installed.

Many of the designs were actually machine-stitched by Dorothy Benson under Rebecca's direction, Singer's were happy to allow much time and trouble to be spent on this project, so Dorothy taught her about different machines, on which she herself was a brilliant technician and interpreter of designs. Some pieces embroidered at this time were white and silver thread on white and off-white silk; others were very colourful.

The outbreak of war in September 1939 and the subsequent changes in the years which followed deeply affected Rebecca particularly as she was still living in London. The devastation of war gravely affected her sensitive nature, and sadly she suffered a complete breakdown. Dorothy Benson of Singer's would visit her in hospital, taking designs and drawings away with her, to be worked on and shown at the next visit. Oswald Crompton was also unwell.

'Adam and Eve'. Various stitches including interlacing.
Derby Museum and Art Gallery

HER DEATH

Rebecca died in August 1947 two years after war had ended. The Obituary in *The Times* began: 'To Mrs Rebecca Crompton, dress designer, embroideress and decorative painter, more than to anybody else belonged the credit of revolutionising the ancient crafts of the needle and bringing them into line with the aims and ideas of modern painting'.

Design by Rebecca Crompton to be carried out in machine embroidery by Dorothy Benson

'Jewelled Swan'

FROM CROYDON TO BROMLEY

That the design and technique of embroidery should have developed with such freedom was due to Rebecca Crompton's unique inspiration coinciding with Elizabeth Grace Thomson's gifts of teaching and her organisational ability at a time when the powers-that-be were very forward looking.

The impact made by these innovations upon the subjects then termed 'Women's Crafts' is difficult to appreciate now, because the present is but an extension of that era. Most of the people doing textile work **now** could trace a remote origin through their tutors back to Croydon or Bromley.

M. E. G. Thomson

Elizabeth Grace Thomson at the entrance to Sidcup School of Art, c 1934

HER FAMILY

The Thomson family home was in Brigstock Road, Thornton Heath, Surrey (now part of the London Borough of Croydon) and this was where Grace and her brother grew up. Their father was a Croydon Councillor in 1912, becoming an Alderman twelve years later. Grace was a student at the Royal Academy Schools, London, and became a proficient painter. Her father, who had by then retired, died in 1929. Her mother moved to Rottingdean, near Brighton, and lived to an old age, latterly being cared for by her daughter. A friend has war-time remembrances of sitting under the shelter-table during air raids over Greater London, with Grace, mother and dog!

TEACHING

On her father's death, Grace found it necessary to find a job. Seeing an advertisement for a part-time post in a private school in Kingswood, near Croydon, she applied and was appointed. The school was for girls up to 13 or 14 and the boys till 9 or 10 years old. A colleague, Dorothy Wilmshurst, teaching craft and nature study at that time, was to work with Grace again some years later. Grace taught the pupils painting and also embroidery, about which at that time she knew nothing. She therefore enrolled at Croydon Art School with Rebecca Crompton, 'to keep a week ahead of the

Left
'Dog in the window', 24 in. x 30 in., worked in an open net material in wool and silk, darning and counted thread stitches

Below left
An exercise using related filling stitches

Below
'Magic Garden', 20 in. x 14 in., c 1937. Superimposed stitching upon plain and patterned materials.
Victoria and Albert Museum

All designed and worked by Rebecca Crompton

pupils' she admitted. She thoroughly enjoyed the experience of being in the embroidery group and was totally intrigued with Rebecca's work. Being a painter she had experience of design and colour and soon graduated from student to part-time helper/ teacher, working both with dress design and embroidery groups.

HER OWN WORK

Grace was also doing her own work. The 1932 exhibition at the V & A Museum showed a piece of work entitled *The Blue Bird*. Her own description of it explains that the background of woollen fabric was actually hand woven: two peasant-type figures are surrounded by birds and flowers, brightly embroidered with a variety of line and filling stitches some using the grain of the basic fabric. The comment by the editor Mrs J. D. Rolleston, in the *Embroideress* magazine of that summer says: ... 'a satisfactory combination of modern design and a high standard of technique. This panel is carried out in rather sharp-coloured blues, cold pinks and green silks on a loosely woven ground. An interesting detail is the muslin apron of the little girl, which is worked separately in shadow stitch and then applied, an innovation at this time'. A friend remembers her work as "always alive", with movement in the design: sometimes this was rigorous, at other times it was more gentle on the eye'.

BROMLEY SCHOOL OF ART

In 1931 or '32, Grace Thomson was appointed to teach embroidery and dress part-time at Bromley School of Art which was in the old Public Library building in Tweedy Road (later to became Bromley College of Art). She travelled there by bus from Croydon, where she continued to live with the Cromptons. At the beginning there were few students and little equipment at Bromley, Kent, but with the valuable support of the Principal, Arthur Baylis Allen and the HMI Mr F. W. Burrows, together with her immense enthusiasm and ability, she made the most unlikely people study seriously. Quite soon some students were taking the Board of Education's Examinations with very good results. Miss Thomson was an outstanding teacher and had a way of concentrating completely on an individual's work, always considering it seriously and saying exactly what she thought. Later when she went round her class, her criticisms were eagerly listened to by those nearby.

She was small and slight with a strong personality, causing everyone to be rather in awe of her. In some ways she had an 'iron hand in a velvet glove.' 'She was a handsome woman, rather too severe for beauty, with fine grey eyes. She became greatly respected and an inspiring teacher. 'I remember her as a kindly encouraging teacher', said a student, 'who because of her obvious interest in embroidery inspired us to design clothes with the extra flair.'

In her early days she did not have quite the presence or confidence of later years and would quietly ask a colleague to help someone with a particular stitch or method that she had forgotten. Her classes were looked forward to as a real experience. When she made her usual entrance, opening wide the doors 'a murmur went around the room'. She was always smartly dressed. One morning she announced that she would read a story, and told the dress people that they were to design ballet costumes based upon the characters in that story.

CHALLENGES

A student remembers being given a challenge: to make a cut paper design by folding it in various ways. The brief was to cut out a tree and place birds within its branches. Her tasks stretched her students' imagination, often specifying figures, animals and birds to be incorporated in the pattern. On other occasions students were taken to visit dress factories and workrooms (before this was usual) which was a valuable experience.

Inevitably the work being done by the students at Bromley was influenced by Croydon, (there was also interchange of staff in the department). Each week the embroidery students had to carry out a test which was criticised constructively, the subjects, and even the designs, were sometimes from the same source.

School of Art, Tweedy Road, Bromley, Kent (formerly the Public Library)

MANY STUDENTS

Grace Thomson was such an inspired and inspiring teacher that her reputation was growing. The numbers were increasing and students would go down to Bromley from the Royal College of Art, one of whom observed: 'E.G.T. had a wonderful gift for encouraging her students by means of unstinted praise. She talked of this to me in her Art School when I was in Bromley a day a week, on my Royal College of Art teaching course. There, I remember that if anyone produced something good, she praised them, as in the case of a small improvement by a struggling student: likewise for someone who came up with just one good idea in an otherwise ordinary piece of work. She believed in plenty of praise wherever possible. She was such a good teacher herself. Her students would produce work at Bromley that one could not do anywhere else at that time'. Other College students, Enid Everard, Lavinia Brown and Eileen Startup (Saunders) attended the classes. Another was Sylvia Green, who wrote that she 'immediately fell under Grace Thomson's spell, the classes were a revelation, I realised that embroidery was a creative and satisfying means of expression. She had a unique gift for making one believe in what one was trying to do'.

Bromley became well known for Women's Crafts, and teachers applied for Sabbatical leave to join the course for a year. She saw the potential in people and helped many to a successful career. Another colleague commented: 'Elizabeth was a hard taskmaster for both students and staff because of her very high standards. Giving unstintingly of herself with energy and originality, engendering such confidence about all that she said and did'.

Yet another colleague recounted that 'she had strong views about colour and personally selected a large stock of various types of threads and background fabrics, feeling that what she had chosen were the most likely to combine to make a satisfactory scheme. Red was considered important – brown and mauvy-red were banned at that time. She liked bright, fresh, exciting colours. Colour theory was disregarded, but tone, hue and proportion should come naturally with any scheme'.

MEETING BERYL DEAN

It was in 1933 that the same H.M.I. advised Beryl Dean, who had been trained at the Royal School of Needlework, to join Grace Thomson's classes, she recognised her outstanding ability as a teacher, and with absolute confidence was converted to the

Dressmaking class, Bromley, c 1937

modern approach towards design, adapting traditional goldwork and other methods to the up-to-date idiom. This technical knowledge was invaluable.

One day an elderly woman came into the school offering for sale some gold threads. These thrilled Beryl, and led her to working her widely exhibited *Madonna* and teaching the technique of goldwork.

As Grace Thomson undertook more and more responsibility and as her reputation and importance grew, the number of students also increased, so Beryl soon was asked to take over more of Grace Thomson's classes. Dress design was of particular appeal to students and to this was added machine embroidery also millinery for which Madame Sheeta came over from Croydon to teach. It was decided also to introduce leatherwork to

'Blue Bird', 13.75 in. square, c 1931. Various line and filling stitches worked by Elizabeth Grace Thomson on loose weave woollen fabric. Embroiderers' Guild Museum Collection

the syllabus and it was suggested that Beryl should experiment, for which a leather machine was produced. Beryl therefore undertook to study for the Board's examinations. Typically Grace Thomson had truly original ideas although she knew nothing about the subject.

Those early days at Bromley were a wonderful opportunity as Grace Thomson was such a very creative artist with a great imagination. She would get to the essentials of any matter and always stressed the importance of constructive criticism. Even then her strong personality was evident: later she became quite a martinet, running her Art Schools in a very disciplined way. Beryl says: 'she could be awe-inspiring and never lacked the courage to say what had to be said. Yet she had a great sense of fun and took an interest in her students, bringing out and developing latent talents in each individual'.

HIGH STANDARDS

A teaching colleague pointed out that 'she was a hard taskmaster, but students responded to this and tried harder. There was lots of unpicking, as all remember! She had such high standards and these were reflected in everything. This was apparent when staging exhibitions. She was determined to improve the image of embroidery, dress and craft subjects. She had an "eye" for display, and much thought lay behind groupings of colours and the placing of items in an exhibition. Much re-arranging went on to get the best effect .... I remember finishing displays and preparing dress shows in my stockinged feet late at night!'.

It is interesting to note that in Rebecca Crompton's exhibition at the Batsford Gallery in 1936, one panel (not for sale as were most of the other pieces) was entitled *Elizabeth not Grace! - To my friend who wishes to change her name.*

In addition to being head of Bromley School of Art she had the responsibility of Sidcup Art School (basically a painting school where she had to introduce crafts rather tactfully), and a little later, at Beckenham School of Art which was added under Baylis Allen's authority. Craft classes were also introduced there.

Her first little house was in Holmdale Road, Chislehurst, which was convenient for both Bromley and Sidcup.

EXHIBITION TIME

In 1937, 'Design in Education' was an important exhibition sponsored by the Board of Education, held in County Hall, Westminster. Baylis Allen and Elizabeth Thomson organised the exhibit of creative embroidery from Kent school children. With help she gave classes twice a week with selected girls from a school in Bexley Heath. Some good work was produced, mainly children's dresses and aprons, attractive materials having been selected for this special project, which was very well displayed, and made a lasting impression upon the teaching of decorative stitchery. The Inspectorate recognised the educational value in giving girls the opportunity to work with colour and textures. The idea for this great project had come from Sir Frank Pick whose vision it was which transformed London Transport and who employed the best artistic and design talents to create the posters under the aegis of the Council for Art and Industry.

The Exhibition illustrated how, by choice of the right materials, the work of elementary schools might show beauty and quality as an introduction to understanding good design. In a letter to the Director of Education in Kent, Frank Pick said: 'I have altogether been surprised at the beauty of the work exhibited and arranged by Baylis Allen and Elizabeth Thomson. I realise both are enthusiasts for the realisation of beauty which counts for so much'. He also thanked the many other people who had worked on this project.

SHORT COURSES

Both Rebecca Crompton and 'Elizabeth' Thomson, as she was now known, continued to instruct the teachers taking the then Board of Education's short courses (assisted from time to time by Beryl Dean). The great trunk of exciting pieces brought up for the embroidery people to use was always eagerly anticipated and Dorothy Allsopp remembers the two leaders making a great impression and can visualise them walking arm in arm, dressed very fashionably, often in brightly coloured outfits, sometimes all in white which was very smart. One of the expeditions was a visit to Broadcasting House, Langham Place. The architecture was very new and modern. Some studios were unusual, for example, there were enormous curtains of black American cloth, a chapel was painted entirely in turquoise blue and covered with gold symbols of many religions, and in a waiting area there was a niche in which was a rubber plant lit from behind (this was 1933), also the repetition of the word SILENCE which made a great impression upon Rebecca Crompton and inspired her to create the huge panel entitled *A Vision of Broadcasting House*. For some time afterwards many students had a craze for outsize embroideries. Some of the display boards made by Iris Hills for one of these courses, to show how fabrics could be pleated and how check fabrics could be enhanced, etc, later became part of the book *Introduction to Practical Embroidery* which the V & A published in the fifties. These courses continued for many years.

STUDENTS AND STAFF

Elizabeth Thomson held special embroidery and design classes for serious students at Bromley. There was always a waiting list, it was considered a privilege to attend. The moment she came into the room the atmosphere seemed to become electric and the people at each table watched her progress down the room. She seemed to enrich the work with the care and thought that she gave it. Of her, at this time, a student teacher at Bromley said: 'Although she did not actually teach me, I remember her as a formidable lady who held herself like a ballet dancer and moved most gracefully, she was always very kind to me as a principal, very efficient and well liked'. (Nora Jones was among the many students.) And at this time there was a good weaving department under Barbara Hoather (one time student of Ethel Mairet of Ditchling, Sussex). Later, Dorothy Wilmshurst, who had worked at the Kingswood school with her, taught book binding and weaving.

Baylis Allen had advised Beryl Dean to take up the Royal Exhibition to the Royal College of Art which she had been awarded, in consequence her teaching at Bromley was curtailed to one afternoon a week and the evenings. During the war she became the acting head of Eastbourne School of Art, and also used to create ballet costumes with the help of the students and designed decor. In 1955, she decided to concentrate upon bringing Ecclesiastical Embroidery up-to-date, undertaking commissions, lecturing, teaching and writing nine books (to date) on the subject, the first she dedicated to *M.E.G. Thomson,* who was very thrilled.

IRIS HILLS JOINS THE TEAM

In the mid-thirties Elizabeth Thomson added to the strength of the team when Iris Hills joined the staff to teach design. Not having been involved with textiles she was impressed by the embroidery and enrolled to learn with Elizabeth. She found working with fabric and thread a very different media from anything she had done before. Later she was to succeed

'Diana', 1930, 15.5 in. x 13.5 in.
Victoria and Albert Museum

'The Breath of Spring', 3 ft x 4 ft. A large wall panel featuring transparent materials

Both designed and worked by
Rebecca Crompton

as head of the department in the Art School also head of the Craft School. Baylis Allen had been appointed as the Regional Head and had much influence in Kent. The new Craft School came under his jurisdiction. It was a detached house nearby and planning the decoration was great fun. The girls responded to the original colour schemes, one said of the green/grey walls: 'It filled me with joyful anticipation'. The floors had to be adapted to withstand the weight of the banks of industrial sewing and embroidery machines. This development was based on an idea for an educational experiment by Elizabeth Thomson and was like the Trade Schools founded at this time. Iris Hills says: 'When I joined Bromley, Miss Thomson had already established a thriving Junior Department, the course was for girls who left Secondary Modern School at 14 years, it was for 2 years, with 2 days general education, to train them to be juniors in the London Couture Dress and Embroidery workrooms. The subjects taught included dressmaking, tailoring, millinery, machine embroidery, tambour beading, hand embroidery, general design, basic lettering and simple display. These girls developed in this atmosphere and responded to working in smaller groups. Firms constantly asked for further juniors to be sent to them. The specialist teachers included Mrs Willey who developed machine embroidery as an art form'.

Iris Hills, also Joan Whayman, taught for about 16 years at Bromley School of Art, which later became Bromley College of Art, and the Craft School. In 1939 a residential course for teachers of Creative Embroidery organised by the Ministry of Education was to be held in Ramsgate. Miss Thomson, with Iris as her assistant having searched London for materials and threads, travelled down by train, followed by all the teachers. They set up the rooms in preparation for starting in the morning. However, being woken early they were amazed to see long lines of teachers making their way back to the station. During the night all teachers had been recalled to their schools - World War II had started!

The Principal died at the beginning of the war and Elizabeth Thomson became acting Principal (so many men having been called up).

'In my first term at the Art School', says Pamela Pavitt, 'the Monday afternoon embroidery class was taken by Miss Thomson - quite daunting for a new student, even more so when she taught me interlacing after a very few weeks. I remember one time joining a group to visit the artist, Mary Kessell's house in Hampstead. On the train back, a friend of mine, who had been a

Bromley student and I sat with Elizabeth Thomson between us. She patted us both on the knees. I felt it was like a mother hen being proud of her chicks!'

INSPECTOR OF WOMEN'S CRAFTS

It was in 1946 that Elizabeth Thomson was appointed the first full-time Inspector of Women's Crafts, for the Ministry of Education. Now she was an Inspector responsible for women's crafts all over the country, which involved much travelling. She learned to drive a car so that it was easier to get around, and Dorothy Wilmshurst was glad to help her friend again and was also interested to hear her speak, and enjoyed experiencing the world of the Inspectorate. She was still missed at Bromley, a student studying machine embroidery there in 1949 can still remember how often Elizabeth Thomson's name was mentioned, almost in hushed tones!

Keith Coleborn was appointed Regional Art Principal and head of Bromley School of Art as from the beginning of the summer term of 1946: he moved from being Principal of the School of Art and Craft, Wallasey, Cheshire. It seems that he was more interested in painting, so the emphasis gradually changed from women's crafts to fine art and from couture design to dress manufacture.

In 1948, Pamela Pavitt remembers, 'Elizabeth Thomson appeared in the secondary classroom where I was teaching my final "specimen lesson" - another daunting day! My first post was in the Art School, part of the Willesden Technical College, North London. Here she was one of the Inspectors who periodically came to see what was being achieved in the Women's Crafts Sphere for which I was responsible. In 1953, after five years there, I changed my job to Hammersmith Day College. This being a college under the London County Council (LCC), Elizabeth Thomson was yet again my Inspector. She took a great interest in my project there, which was very much in keeping with her desire to bring beauty and creativity to youngsters who were receiving one day's education each week when released from their jobs. These included many workers from Lyons' Bakery in that area and juniors from the Post Office Savings Bank. It was her idea that I should teach there to help to reinforce her wish to achieve high standards for everyone (which had been the driving force for the 1937 exhibition *Design in Education)*. She showed concern for these standards in many areas of education and community work in London. One of the

Willesden students was interviewed by Elizabeth Thomson to find out whether she was interested to teach crafts within Holloway Prison. In the end it did not work out for her, but it did for others.'

NEEDLEWORK DEVELOPMENT SCHEME (NDS)

Among her other and varied duties was Elizabeth's connection with the NDS, in which she became very involved. This was sponsored by J & P Coats of Glasgow and promoted by Colin Martin (through whom the Scandinavian influence was introduced). When it started in 1934 the aim was to encourage greater interest in embroidery and to raise the standard of design. This work was originally for Scotland. It closed during the war, but opened again in 1944 in England as well as Scotland, with an advisory council being set up in 1946. The scheme possessed a good collection of embroideries and planned publications which would help secondary schools and other interested institutes.

Elizabeth Thomson was on the Advisory Council which also included a representative from the V & A, a Scottish Educationalist, the 'Expert in charge', and Colin Martin representing Coats. As this scheme would have such an influence on embroidery in education, she was insistent on good standards for all aspects of their work - the embroidery selection, the presentation and production of information. All samples to be added to the collection had to be accepted by Elizabeth Thomson, otherwise they were returned. Termly Bulletins were sent out to all schools; other booklets were also published, *And So to Sew* and *And So to Embroider*, the standard checked by Elizabeth Thomson's 'beady' eye. It was to encourage people constructively to attempt to do their own designs that many specimens were prepared which showed pattern contrived from the arrangement of striped, checked and spotted, also printed cottons.

An ex-student who worked for NDS in Glasgow said: 'A series of leaflets and bulletins was being produced to show what could be done creatively in embroidery and needlework. Approval was being sought for these schemes from the Ministry of Education, where Miss Thomson was now on the Inspectorate, because they would be circulated to many schools. So I was sent to London to discuss the project and she was a great help to me. I think I was granted an interview in the first place because she knew me from Bromley Art School.' The bulletins were finally approved and sent out to all the schools as a great assistance to teachers, and raised the standard and excitement in embroidery and needlework. Elizabeth Thomson was closely involved with the NDS and its special project on Embroidery Design. It was planned that completely new ideas and designs were to be interpreted, some by hand and others by machine, whichever method seemed to be the better. Finally the Arts Council would mount an exhibition of all work that had been done.

Mary Kessell, a sensitive painter and draughtsman, was chosen by the NDS in 1946 to become involved in the project, initially trying her hand at stitchery but latterly working with skilled hand and machine embroiderers. Much had been achieved by 1948, but to increase the number of specimens for a future exhibition, more time had to be diverted to the task. A full-time machine embroiderer (Frances Gibb) and a large group of hand workers, including children at the County Grammar School for Girls, Bromley, under Marion Campbell, all set to work to have many more samples ready. It was early the following year that the exhibition was mounted by the Arts Council of Great Britain at Holborn Town Hall, London. From the catalogue *An Experiment in Embroidery Design*, it states: '...it is refreshing to find new ideas infused into the craft of embroidery, for which this country has been justly famed in the past and in which our technical skill remains high'.

Dorothy Allsopp was the Expert in Charge of the NDS from 1949 to 1954, followed by Iris Hills, until the scheme closed in the early sixties. Both these leaders knew Elizabeth well and met her often.

Elizabeth Grace Thomson opening Beryl Dean's (left) exhibition in 1958 (Margaret Nicolson at back)

'My Mother', 24 in. x 18 in., c 1930/35. Carried out in hand embroidery stitches by Elizabeth Grace Thomson, upon loose weave woollen fabric. Embroiderers' Guild Museum Collection

'Chords', 34.75 in. x 35.5 in., c 1934, by Elizabeth Grace Thomson. Appliqué combined with embroidery (now very faded). Embroiderers' Guild Museum Collection

THE ILEA INSPECTOR

All Elizabeth Thomson's work as an inspector was concerned with high standards, good taste, and craftmanship throughout the country. But after seven years of this responsibility, she was happier to change to the London County Council (later the ILEA) which was of equal importance with her work for the Ministry of Education. Her subjects were Women's Crafts in Further and Higher Education and her interest was shown widely and on many courses. She was also concerned with social issues which included interest in the women in Holloway Prison, London. She felt strongly that everybody should have the chance of handling beautiful things.

HER RETIREMENT

Elizabeth retired in 1961 to an interesting house 'Roughdown', Kingston, near Lewes. She has left little work for posterity, partly because she had such high standards that she destroyed many earlier pieces by having a great bonfire because they did not match up to her ideals. She said that she 'didn't want stuff lying around'. As her nephew said: 'She was very modest, and did not make a lot of her talents to others'. There are a few examples of hers and of Rebecca Crompton's work in the Embroiderers' Guild Collection, but she has left a great wealth of ideas in the minds of those who knew her, also those she taught. She set very high standards by which to assess creative work. It is all reflected in the quotation: 'Her greatest contribution to Women's Crafts was her determination that they should be taken seriously and upgraded educationally. She did not consider the work should be accepted as something trivial. She felt that all creative crafts should be respected in their own right. They should be given all the time and care in presentation which is given to choosing the right mount and frame for a painting'.

In 1982, at the age of 82, Elizabeth Grace Thomson died after suffering another heart attack.

In Retrospect

Having prepared the way for experimental embroidery, and having had their ideas tested and accepted by the education authorities, we can see, in retrospect, the importance of the work of these two indominatable women who have encouraged and inspired other now notable teachers to continue their pioneering work.

No longer are school children confined to the laborious making of unusable objects. Out comes the 'bit bag' containing fabrics of exciting colours and textures from which to choose and from which to create all sorts of interesting items; and the previously confined embroidery techniques of the art student has given to the freedom of stitchery and the acceptance of embroidery as an art form, being exhibited in galleries alongside fine art paintings and sculpture, and reinforced by the award of the MA degree in 1962.

In 1995 the hundredth anniversary of the birth of both Rebecca Crompton and Elizabeth Grace Thomson was commemorated by an exhibition of their work entitled 'Freedom to Stitch' at the Embroiderers Guild at Hampton Court. In their Spring 1995 magazine, their curator, Lynn Szygenda, writes: 'Surviving embroideries by Crompton and Thomson reveal a varied repertoire of stitches, including machine techniques in Crompton's work, but all carefully selected to achieve the aims of the design. In their teaching and example, Rebecca Crompton and Elizabeth Grace Thomson were amongst a band of embroiderers who resurrected embroidery, and in releasing it from the dictates of technical perfection gave it the freedom to grow into an expressive art form which the contemporary embroidery in *Freedom to Stitch* and *Art of the Stitch* will confirm.'